Addie Guthrie Weaver

The Story of our Flag, colonial and national

Addie Guthrie Weaver

The Story of our Flag, colonial and national

ISBN/EAN: 9783337154059

Printed in Europe, USA, Canada, Australia, Japan

Cover: Foto ©ninafisch / pixelio.de

More available books at **www.hansebooks.com**

The Story of Our Flag.

Colonial and National,

with Historical Sketch

of

The Quakeress Betsy Ross

By

Addie Guthrie Weaver.

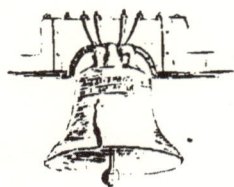

Colored
Illustrations
of the Flags and
Washington's Coat of Arms
By the Author

Preface.

For some years the Author has been interested in the history of our First Flag and its fair maker, Betsy Ross, and fortunately, through a family relationship with one of the descendants, became familiar with much of the family history.

It seemed that so beautiful and estimable a lady, and one who played so important a part in those stirring events of our early history should be better known and appreciated by her sisters of to-day.

Fitting, it seems, that while man in defending our Flag has accomplished his greatest achievements, and won undying fame, woman first fashioned into "a thing of beauty" the symbol of that patriotic devotion.

To Mr. George Canby of Philadelphia, and Mrs. Sophia Campion Guthrie of Washington, D. C., grandson and great granddaughter, respectively, of Betsy Ross, the author is indebted for family history that has inspired this work, and to them and other descendants, this book is affectionately dedicated by

THE AUTHOR.

Flag House of Betsey Ross. 239 Arch St. Philadelphia

Sketched by
Helen Hayes.

The Story of Our Flag.

COLONIAL AND NATIONAL.

The history of our flag from its inception, in fact, the inception itself, has been a source of much argument and great diversity of opinion. Many theories and mystifications have gone forth, mingled with a few facts, giving just enough color of truth to make them seem plausible. It is for the purpose of clearing away the veil of doubt that hangs around the origin of the Stars and Stripes that this book has been written.

The Continental Congress in 1775 was very much disturbed over the embarrassing situation of the colonies, and after Washington was appointed Commander-in-Chief of the Army, it showed its independence by appointing a committee composed of Benjamin Franklin, Benjamin Harrison and Mr. Lynch to create a colonial flag that would be national in its tendency. They finally decided on one with thirteen bars, alternate red and white, the "King's Colors" with the crosses of St. Andrew and St. George in a field of blue. The cross of St. Andrew then, as now, was of white, while the cross of St. George was of red. The colonies still acknowledged the sovereignty of England—as this flag attested—but united against her tyranny. This was known as the "flag of our union"- -that is, the union of the colonies, and was not created until after the committee had been to the camp at Cambridge and consulted with Washington. It was probably made either at the camp at Cambridge or in Boston, as it was unfurled by Washington under the Charter Oak on January 2, 1776. It received thirteen cheers and a salute of thirteen guns.

It is not known whether Samuel Adams, the "Father of Liberty," was consulted in regard to this flag, but it is a well known fact that he was looking forward, even then, to the independence of the colonies, while Washington, Franklin and the others still looked for justice,—tardy though it might be,—from England.

Two days later, on the 4th of January, 1776, Washington received the King's speech, and as it happened to come so near to the time of the adoption of the new flag, with the English crosses of St. Andrew and St. George, many of the regulars thought it meant submission, and the English seemed for the time to so understand it; but our army showed great indignation over the King's speech to parliament, and burned all of the copies.

In a letter of General Washington to Joseph Reed, written January 4, he says: "We are at length favored with the sight of his majesty's most gracious speech, breathing sentiments of tenderness and compassion for his deluded American subjects. The speech I send you (a volume of them were sent out by the Boston gentry) was farcical enough and gave great joy to them without knowing or intending it, for on that day (the 2nd) which gave being to our new army, but before the proclamation came to hand, we hoisted the Union flag, in compliment to the United Colonies, but behold it was received at Boston as a token of the deep impression the speech had made upon us and as a signal of submission. By this time I presume they begin to think it strange that we have not made a formal surrender of our lines."

At this time the number and kinds of flags that were in use on land and sea, were only limited to the ingenuity of the state and military officials. This was very embarrassing. On May 20, 1776, Washington was requested to appear before Congress on important secret military business. Major-General Putnam, according to Washington's letters, was left in command at New York during his absence. It was in the latter part of May, 1776, that Washington, accompanied by Colonel George Ross, a member of his staff, and by the Honorable Robert Morris, the great financier of the revolution, called upon Mrs. Betsy Ross, a niece of Colonel Ross. She was a young and beautiful widow, only twenty-four years of age, and known to be expert at needle work. They called to engage her services in preparing our first starry flag. She lived in a little house in Arch street, Philadelphia,

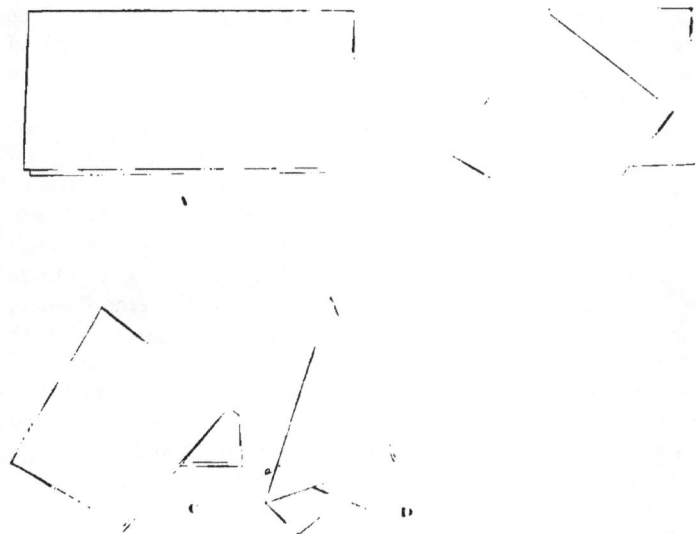

which stands to-day unchanged, with the exception of one large window, which has been placed in the front. It was here, in this house, that Washington unfolded a paper on which had been rudely sketched a plan of a flag of thirteen stripes, with a blue field dotted with thirteen stars. They talked over the plan of this flag in detail, and Mrs. Ross noticed that the stars which were sketched were six-pointed, and suggested that they should have five points. Washington admitted that she was correct, but he preferred a star that would not be an exact copy of that on his coat of arms, and he also thought that a six-pointed star would be easier to cut. Mrs. Ross liked the five-pointed star, and to show that they were easily cut she deftly folded a piece of paper and with one clip of her scissors unfolded a perfect star with five points. (See illustration showing the way Betsy Ross folded the paper giving the five-pointed star which has ever since graced our country's banner. A, first fold of a square piece of paper; B, second; C, third, and D, fourth fold. The dotted line AA is the clip of the scissors.

There is no record that Congress took any action on the national colors at this session,—but this first flag was made by Betsy Ross at this time, and in this way, and we find in Washington's letter of May 28, 1776, to General Putnam at New York, positive instructions "to the several colonels to hurry to get their colors done." In the orderly book, May 31, 1776, are these words: "General Washington has written to General Putnam desiring him in the most pressing terms, to give positive orders to all the colonels to have colors immediately completed for their respective regiments." The proof is positive that the committee approved the finished flag of Betsy Ross, and she was instructed to procure all the bunting possible in Philadelphia and make flags for the use of congress, Colonel Ross furnishing the money.

It is easily understood how on account of the meager resources of Congress and the unsettled condition of affairs generally, together with the fact that legislative action was extremely slow and tedious, that Colonel Ross should expedite matters by defraying the expense of this first order for our national colors. There is little, if any, doubt but that Washington on December 24th, Christmas Eve, in 1776, carried the starry flag in making that perilous trip through ice and snow across the Delaware, leading his sturdy, but poorly equipped troops. How inspiring to look back to that night when the Massachusetts fishermen so skilfully managed the boats that the whole army was safely landed and in line of march at four o'clock on Christmas morning. The story of how they plodded on through ice and snow, surprising and defeating the Hessians and capturing a thousand men and their ammunition and equipments, is well known. This was the battle of Trenton, which changed the whole aspect of the war, even causing Lord Cornwallis to disembark and again start in pursuit of Washington, whose cause he had so lately declared lost. It is fitting here to speak of that friend of Washington. Robert Morris, one of the committee that originated our national colors, the great patriot who after the battle of Trenton went from house to house, soliciting money from his friends to clothe and feed this glorious army, which had fought so well.

Congress was very slow to act, and did not seem able to command even the meager resources of the different colonies. It lacked the centralized government which gives it such strength to-day. Considering the grave questions affecting the life and liberty of the people, it is not strange that the flag or any definite action regarding it, was not given prompt consideration. To indicate how slow Congress was to act in regard to the flag, we have only to refer to the Congressional records, which show that the resolution for its adoption was dated over one year after it was actually created, by the committee of which Washington was chief; that is on June 14, 1777. However, a month previous to this, Congress sent Betsy Ross an order on the treasury for £14, 12s, 2d., for flags for the fleet in the Delaware River, and she soon received an order to make all the government flags. The first flag was made of English bunting, exactly the same as those of to-day, excepting that our bunting now is of home manufacture.

There seems to be no question but that these colors, the stars and stripes, were unofficially adopted immediately after the completion of the first flag, the latter part of May, 1776, and that they went into general use at once, so far as it was practicable under the conditions then existing. Washington had the first flag created at this time. It was satisfactory, and he immediately instructed General Putnam to have the colonels prepare their colors—the colors that had just been approved, and which we know to be our flag of to-day.

The first reference we have of an English description of our flag is at the surrender of General Burgoyne, October 17, 1777, when one of the officers said: "The stars of the new flag represent a constellation of states."

Mr. George Canby, an estimable gentleman of the old school, and a grandson of Betsy Ross, has been tireless and indefatigable in his researches on the subject of our flag, and he claims, as did his brother, Mr. William J. Canby, before him, that the first flag with stars and stripes went into immediate use after its inception in the latter part of May, 1776.

The Declaration of Independence was passed by Congress on July 4, 1776, and some authorities, of whom Admiral Preble is the best, seem to infer that the Cambridge flag, with its English crosses, which was unfurled by Washington under the Charter Oak, was still carried by our armies until Congress took action in 1777. That Washington or Congress would sanction the carrying of this flag after the Declaration of Independence seems absurd, and it is certainly against all proof, as well as against the records of the family whose ancestor made the first flag.

Peale's portrait of Washington at the battle of Trenton, December 26 and 27, 1776, shows the Union Jack with the thirteen stars in the field of blue. Admiral Preble says, this is "only presumptive proof" that the stars were at that time in use on our flag, but Titian R. Peale, son of the painter, says: "I visited the Smithsonian Institute to see the portrait of Washington painted by my father after the battle of Trenton. The flag represented has a blue field with white stars arranged in a circle. I don't know that I ever heard my father speak of that flag, but the trophies at Washington's feet I know he painted from the flags then captured, and which were left with him for the purpose." He further says: "He was always very particular in the matters of historic record in his pictures."

This Preble admits in his book, but evidently thought that the artist, Peale, took the flag as it was then (1779), and not the flag of 1776, which the writer claims was identically the same Through persistent research many facts have come to light that would doubtless have changed the opinion of the late Admiral Preble—facts that were unknown to him.

On Saturday, June 14, 1777, Congress finally officially adopted the flag of our Union and independence, to-wit:

Resolved, "That the flag of the thirteen United States be thirteen stripes, alternate red and white; that the Union be thirteen stars, white in the blue field, representing a new constellation."

There is not the slightest record in any of the mss. journals in the library of Congress, or in the original files or in the drafts in motions made in the continental Congress of any previous legislative action for the establishment of a national flag for the United States of America, whose independence was declared nearly a year previous. Even after the official adoption of the flag it was not thoroughly brought before the people for many months. All of this adds to the proof that Congress was simply adopting and legalizing a flag that was in general use. That there was no recorded discussion in Congress regarding the adoption of our flag, was perfectly natural, because the star spangled banner came in with our independence, and at this time (June 14, 1777) was simply being officially acknowledged.

There is some diversity of opinion as to how the red, white and blue arranged in the stars and stripes came to be thought of as our flag.

The flag of the Netherlands, which is of red, white and blue stripes, had been familiar to the pilgrims while they lived in Holland, and its three stripes of red, white and blue were doubtless not forgotten. But it seems most probable that the coat of arms of the Washington family furnished more than a suggestion. The coat of arms of his ancestors, that had been adopted by him, comprised the red, white and blue and the stars, and was familiar to all who were associated with Washington. He it was who brought the pencil drawing, when, with the others, he called upon Mrs. Ross to have a suitable flag made, and as we find no mention in history, records or diaries as to who made the drawing, it seems conclusive that he himself designed and drew the plan from his own coat of arms, which was entirely different from England's colors which had become necessarily distasteful.

It seems fitting in this place to write a little history in regard to the Washington coat of arms, the earliest mention of which was by Lawrence Washington, worshipful mayor of Northampton, England, in 1532. In 1540 he placed it upon the porch of his manor house, and on the tomb of Ann, his wife, in 1564. At the old church at Brighton, England, the tombs of Washington's ancestors are marked by memorial plates of brass bearing the arms of the family, which consisted of a shield that bore the stars and stripes. The Archeological Society of England, the highest authority on ancient churches and heraldic matters, states that from the red and white bars, and stars of this shield, and the raven issuant from its crest (borne later by General Washington), the framers of the constitution took their idea of the flag.

When General Washington's great-grandfather, Sir John Washington, came to this country in 1657, the family shield was brought with him. Sir John settled in Virginia, and established the American line of Washingtons. George Washington afterwards had it emblazoned upon the panels of his carriages, on his watch seals, book marks, and his dishes also bore the same emblem.

EXITUS ACTA PROBAT

WASHINGTON COAT OF ARMS.

The accompanying plate shows the form and colors of the Coat of Arms of the Washington family, back as early as 1300.

The name first appeared as De Wessynton; then Weshyngton, and, finally, Washington.

How appropriately our own beautiful shield of the United States comes in here, and why not? was he not the "Father of Our Country"? and what more natural than that he should have left the imprint of his life and characteristics in symbol?

The central figure is a fac-simile of his book plate.

After the admission of Vermont and Kentucky into the Union, Congress passed an act in 1794, increasing both the stars and stripes from thirteen to fifteen, to take effect May, 1795. It was as follows:

"An act making alterations in the flag of the United States. Be it enacted, etc., That from and after the first day of May, one thousand, seven hundred and ninety-five, the flag of the United States be fifteen stripes, alternate red and white, and that the union be fifteen stars, white in a blue field.

"Approved January 13. 1794."

This flag was used for several years. It flew at the mastheads of our gallant ships and was carried by our little army in the war with England in 1812. A few years later Tennessee, Ohio, Louisiana and Indiana, now won to civilization by hardy pioneers, clamored for admittance into the Union. When they were finally admitted as states, another change in the flag became necessary. The sturdy young republic was advancing by leaps and bounds in civilization and wealth; its hardy sons pushing further west and south constantly, reclaiming from wild savages, to the uses of their own race, greater and larger areas, which were bound to be erected into states and take their places in the family of the original thirteen. It became manifest that legislation was necessary, permanently defining the national flag, and providing for such changes as the future development of the country would require. Congress rose to the occasion. A committee, with Hon. Peter Wendover of New York as chairman, was appointed to frame a law, and with very little delay the committee reported a measure fulfilling every requirement then existing, and providing for all the future. The measure was passed by congress and went on the statute books as the law establishing the flag as our great-grandfathers of that day knew it, and as we know it to-day. The law has never been changed, and here it is:

"An act to establish the flag of the United States.

"Section 1. Be it enacted, etc., That from and after the fourth day of July next, the flag of the United States be thirteen horizontal stripes, alternate red and white; that the Union have twenty stars, white in the blue field.

"Sec. 2. And be it further enacted, That on the admission of every new state into the Union, one star be added to the union of the flag, and that such addition shall take effect on the fourth of July next succeeding such admission. Approved April 4, 1818."

The thirteen stripes will always represent the number of the "old thirteen" whose patriotism and love of justice brought about the independence of America. The stars that come into the blue sky of the flag will mark or indicate the increase of the states since the adoption of the Constitution. It is interesting to note that under the stars and stripes Washington, in 1793, laid the corner stone of the capitol of the United States, first having personally selected the site of the building. It is also interesting to know that Washington did not live to see the capitol completed, but died before the seat of government was moved to Washington in 1800. The main capitol building was not completed till 1811. It is also a matter of historical interest that the president's home, now called the White House, was completed during the life of Washington, and it is an authenticated fact that he and his wife inspected the house in all its parts only a few days before his death. The president's house was practically destroyed by the British in 1814; the walls alone remained intact, but the stone was so discolored that when the building was reconstructed, it had to be painted, and from this came the name of the "White House."

The large picture of Washington, by Stewart, which is now in the east room, at the time of the bombardment by the British, was taken out of its frame by Mrs. Dolly Madison, wife of the president, and sent to a secure place across the river.

2

This flag of forty-five stars, this flag of our country, is our inspiration. It kindles in our hearts patriotic feelings, it carries our thoughts and our minds forward in the cause of liberty and right. On sea and on land, wherever the star spangled banner waves, it thrills the heart of every true American with pride. It recalls the memories of battles bravely fought. It recalls the victories of Trenton and Princeton, it recalls the victories of Gettysburg and Appomattox. We see the flag as first carried by Paul Jones across the sea; we see the flag as carried by Commodore Perry on Lake Erie; we see the flag as carried by Farragut at New Orleans; we see Admiral Dewey through smoke and fire hoisting the flag in the Philippines. This same flag was carried to victory by Admirals Sampson and Schley in Cuba. This flag recalls the many battles bravely fought and grandly won. It symbolizes the principles of human progress and human liberty. The stars represent the unity and harmony of our states. They are the constellation of our country. Their luster reflects to every nation of the world. The flag of 1776, the old thirteen, has grown to be one of the great flags of the earth. Its stars reach from ocean to ocean. We see it leading the armies of Washington and Greene, of Grant and Sherman and Sheridan, and of Miles, Shafter and Merritt.

This is the flag of the "dawn's early light" that was immortalized by Francis Scott Key—"The Star Spangled Banner."

General Grant once said, "No one is great enough to write his name on the flag."

A century under the stars and stripes has been the greatest century of progress in the history of the world. No other nation that has ever existed has carried forward such a banner. Its colors were taken from various sources and brought into one harmonious combination, and it "waves over a country which unites all nationalities and all races, and in the end brings about a homogeneous population, representing the highest type of civilization." It is not strange that this flag of Washington, of Hamilton, of Adams, of Jefferson; this flag of Jackson, of Webster, of Clay, this flag of Lincoln, of Grant and of McKinley should exert such world-wide influence. It holds a unique place in the nations of the world. It has spread knowledge and faith and hope among all classes. It means liberty with justice. Its international influence places it in the first rank. It twines itself among the flags of other nations, not for destruction or war, but for friendship and progress in the cause of humanity. In the councils of peace; in the conquests of war; in everything that pertains to government, in everything that pertains to the advancement of humanity, it calls forth the admiration of mankind. Under its influence the arts and sciences have been fostered, commerce has expanded and education has been made universal. It waves for the right and the harbors of the globe will salute this banner as a harbinger of progress and peace.

The youngest nation has the oldest flag.

It is of historical interest that our flag is older than the present flag of Great Britain, which was adopted in 1801, and it is nine years older than the flag of Spain, which was adopted in 1785. The French tricolor was decreed in 1794; then comes the flag of Portugal in 1830; then the Italian tricolor in 1848; then the flags of the old empires of China and Japan, and of the empire of Germany, which represents the sovereignty of fourteen distinct states established in 1870.

Prior to the Revolution, and indeed during the evolution of a nation through the crucible of war, separate and distinct flags were popular with the colonists. Nearly every colony had at least one. They were not abandoned until it became apparent the colonies were never again to be colonies, but to form a nation with one flag, one set of institutions and laws, a fact which inspired the visit of Washington to Betsy Ross as told in the foreging papers. Many of the colonial flags were interesting.

GROUP OF COLONIAL FLAGS, NO. 1.

The two upper flags of this group represent those used at Bunker Hill July 18, 1775, and bore these inscriptions: On one side, "An Appeal to Heaven," and on the other, "Qui Transtulit Sustinet"—He who transported will sustain.

These were beautiful flags, and research shows that both colors were used.

Trumbull gives the red in his celebrated painting in the capitol at Washington, and other authentic accounts show that the blue flag was carried also—the color being the only difference in the two.

THE PINE TREE FLAG.

The pine tree flag which was a favorite with the officers of the American privateers, had a white field with a green pine tree in the middle and bore the motto, "An appeal to heaven."

This flag was officially endorsed by the Massachusetts council, which in April, 1776, passed a series of resolutions providing for the regulation of the sea service, among which was the following:

Resolved, That the uniform of the officers be green and white, and that they furnish themselves accordingly, and that the colors be a white flag with a green pine tree and the inscription, "An appeal to heaven."—Harper's Round Table.

AN APPEAL TO HEAVEN

DON'T TREAD ON ME

CONQUER OR DIE

LIBERTY

The striped Continental flag opposite the pine tree flag was of red and white stripes without a field.

THE RATTLESNAKE FLAG.

The device of a rattlesnake was popular among the colonists, and its origin as an American emblem is a curious feature in our national history.

It has been stated, that its use grew out of a humorous suggestion made by a writer in Franklin's paper—the Pennsylvania Gazette—that, in return for the wrongs which England was forcing upon the colonists, a cargo of rattlesnakes should be sent to the mother country and "distributed in St. James' Park, Spring Garden and other places of pleasure."

Colonel Gadsden, one of the marine committee, presented to Congress, on the 8th of February, 1776, "an elegant standard, such as is to be used by the commander-in-chief of the American navy; being a yellow flag with a representation of a rattlesnake coiled for attack."

WASHINGTON LIFE GUARD FLAG.

There is probably no more interesting revolutionary flag than this. The Washington Life Guard was organized in 1776, soon after the siege of Boston, while the American army was encamped near New York.

It was said to have been in the museum at Alexandria, Va., which was burned soon after the war of the rebellion, and nearly everything lost. It was of white silk with the design painted on it.

The uniform of the guard was as follows: blue coat with white facings, white waistcoat and breeches, with blue half gaiters, a cocked hat and white plume.

THE GRAND UNION FLAG.

These were the colors selected by Franklin, Harrison and Lynch, and unfurled by Washington under the Charter Oak, January 2, 1776, and hereafter described.

The flag of the Richmond Rifles follows with the one used at Moultrie.

The latter was of blue with white crescent in the dexter corner and was used by Colonel Moultrie, September 13, 1775, when he received orders from the Council of Safety for taking Fort Johnson on James Island, South Carolina.

In the early years of the Revolution, a number of emblems were in use which became famous. The standard on the southeast bastion of Fort Sullivan (or Moultrie, as it was afterward named), on June 28, 1776, by Colonel Moultrie, was a blue flag with a white crescent in the upper left hand corner, and the word "Liberty" in white letters emblazoned upon it.

This was the flag that fell outside the fort and was secured by Sergeant Jasper, who leaped the parapet, walked the whole length of the fort, seized the flag, fastened it to a sponge staff and in sight of the whole British fleet and in the midst of a perfect hail of bullets planted it firmly upon the bastion. The next day Governor Rutledge visited the fort and rewarded him by giving him his sword.

Then comes the flag of White Plains, October 28, 1776, with little historical importance.

The flag made by Betsy Ross, under the direction of General Washington, Robert Morris, and Colonel George Ross, consisted of thirteen bars, alternate red and white, with a circle of thirteen stars in the field of blue.

LIBERTY OR DEATH

LIBERTY TREE

AN APPEAL

TO GOD

COUNT PULASKI'S FLAG.

The Moravian sisters of Bethlehem, Pennsylvania, gave to Count Pulaski's corps, which he had previously organized at Baltimore and which was called "Pulaski's Legion," a beautiful crimson silk banner, embroidered in yellow silk and sent it with their blessing. Pulaski was at this time suffering from a wound, and was on a visit to Lafayette, whose headquarters were at Bethlehem. Count Pulaski was a Polish patriot, born March 4, 1747. After having bravely fought for Poland with his father and brothers until the Polish cause became hopeless, he came to America, arriving in Philadelphia in 1777. He entered the army as a volunteer, but performing such brave service at Brandywine, he was promoted to the command of cavalry with rank of brigadier-general. In 1778 Congress gave him leave to raise a body of men under his own command. Longfellow has most beautifully described the presentation of the flag in verse. Pulaski bore this flag to victory through many battles until he fell mortally wounded at Savannah, October 14, 1779. The banner was saved by his first lieutenant, who received fourteen wounds, and delivered it to Captain Bentalon, who on retiring from the army, took it home to Baltimore. It was carried in the procession which welcomed Lafayette in 1824, and was then deposited in the Peale Museum. In 1844 Mr. Edmund Peale presented it to the Historical Society of Maryland, where it is now preserved in a glass case. These are interesting historical facts.

Flag of red and blue bars with serpent stretched across and words, "Don't Tread on Me."

Another flag of white, with blue bands top and bottom and a pine tree in center, with the inscriptions: Liberty Tree and An Appeal to Heaven.

THE "DON'T TREAD ON ME" FLAG.

Another use of the rattlesnake was upon a ground of thirteen horizontal bars alternate red and white, the snake extending diagonally across the stripes, and the lower white stripes bearing the motto—"Don't Tread on Me." The snake was always represented as having thirteen rattles, and the number thirteen seems constantly to have been kept in mind. Thus, thirteen vessels are ordered to be built; thirteen stripes are placed on the flag; in one design thirteen arrows are grasped in a mailed hand; and in a later one thirteen arrows are in the talons of an eagle.

ANOTHER "DON'T TREAD ON ME" FLAG.

One of the favorite flags also was of white with a pine tree in the center. The words at the top were "An Appeal to God," and underneath the snake were the words, "Don't Tread on Me." Several of the companies of minute men adopted a similar flag, giving the name of their company with the motto "Liberty or Death." This flag is familiar to the public as the annual celebrations bring out descriptions of it in the press.

THE PRESIDENT'S FLAG.

Within the last few years special flags have been designed for the President, the Secretary of the Navy and Secretary of War. The President's flag is a very beautiful blue banner, in the center of which is a spread eagle bearing the United States shield on its breast, with the thirteen stars in a half circle overhead. It is flown at the main mast-head of naval vessels while the President remains on board, and on being hoisted it is the signal for the firing of the President's salute.

COLONIAL AND PATRIOTIC MUSIC.

The colonial music was mostly borrowed and adapted to the occasion. The Pilgrims had more important duties to perform and in those years of stirring events no one was in a mood to write music.

The first song to be used was that old and familiar one, "Yankee Doodle." It made a powerful rallying cry in calling to arms against England. It is so old that it is impossible to decide just where the term came from.

It has been traced back to Greece—"Iankhe Doule," meaning "Rejoice, O Slave," and to the Chinese—"Yong Kee," meaning "Flag of the Ocean." It is said the Persians called Americans "Yanki Doon'iah," "Inhabitants of the New World." The Indians too, come in for their share of the credit of originating the term, as the Cherokee word "Eankke," which means "coward" and "slave," was often bestowed upon the inhabitants of New England.

At the time of the uprising against Charles the First, Oliver Cromwell rode into Oxford, on an insignificant little horse, wearing a single plume in a knot called a "macaroni." The song was sung derisively by the cavaliers at that time. The tune is said to have come from Spain or France, there being several versions of the words.

It came into play when our ancestors flocked into Ticonderoga in answer to the call of Abercrombie. At that early day no one refused, but all answered the call and came equipped as best they could, but hardly any two alike, and to the trained English regulars must have presented a ridiculous appearance. Dr. Shamburg changed the words of the old satire to fit the new occasion. But in less than a year it was turned by the Yankees against the English in the form of a rallying cry and possessed new meaning.

History had emphasized it, and with the accompaniment of the shrill pipe and half worn drum calling the simple cottagers together, it must have aroused all their noble and sturdy patriotism.

Who that has viewed that stirring picture in the Corcoran Art Gallery at Washington, "Yankee Doodle," could fail to catch the inspiration of the scene. The old man with his thin grey locks, but head erect and face glowing with enthusiasm as he keeps time to the old tune, followed by the small boy with his drum. One scarcely knows whether humor or pathos predominates; but certain we are that all alike stepped to its chords; it found an answering echo in each heart and led them on to glory.

YANKEE DOODLE.

Father and I went down to camp.
Along with Captain Goodwin,
And there we saw the men and boys
As thick as hasty pudding.

CHORUS.

Yankee Doodle, keep it up.
Yankee doodle dandy;
Mind the music and the step.
And with the girls be handy.

And there was Captain Washington,
Upon a slapping stallion.
A giving orders to his men.
I guess there was a million.—Cho.

And then the feathers on his hat.
They looked so tarnal finey.
I wanted peskily to get
To give to my Jemima.—Cho.

And there they had a swamping gun,
As big as a log of maple,
On a duced little cart.
A load for father's cattle.—Cho.

And every time they fired it off
    It took a horn of powder;
It made a noise like father's gun,
    Only a ration louder.—Cho.

I went as near to it myself
    As Jacob's underpinin',
And father went as near again,
    I th't the duce was in him.—Cho.

It scared me so, I ran the streets,
    Nor stopped as I remember,
Till I got home and safely locked
    In granny's little chamber.—Cho.

And there I see a little keg,
    Its heads were made of leather;
They knocked upon it with little sticks
    To call the folks together.—Cho.

And then they'd fife away like fun
    And play on corn-stalk fiddles;
And some had ribbons red as blood
    All bound around their middles.—Cho.

The troopers, too, would gallop up,
    And fire right in our faces;
It scared me almost to death
    To see them run such races.—Cho.

Uncle Sam came there to change
    Some pancakes and some onions,
For 'lasses cake to carry home
    To give his wife and young ones.—Cho.

But I can't tell you half I see,
    They keep up such a smother;
So I took off my hat, made a bow,
    And scampered off to mother."—Cho.

AMERICA.

Rev. Samuel Francis Smith was born in Boston October 21, 1808, and graduated in the class of '29 from Harvard University. He enjoyed the honor of having for his classmate Oliver Wendell Holmes, in whose beautiful poem, entitled "The Boys," the name of the author of "America" is affectionately mentioned.

> And there's a nice youngster of excellent pith;
> Fate tried to conceal him by naming him Smith,
> But he shouted a song for the brave and the free,
> Just read on his medal—"My Country of Thee"!

"America" was written in 1832, the tune being the old one of "God Save the Queen," and first rendered on the 4th of July of the same year by the children of Park St. Church, Boston.

AMERICA.

My country, 'tis of thee,
Sweet land of liberty,
  Of thee I sing!
Land where my fathers died,
Land of the pilgrims' pride,
From every mountain side
  Let freedom ring.

My native country, thee—
Land of the noble free,
  Thy name I love,
I love thy rocks and rills,
Thy woods and templed hills,
My heart with rapture thrills
  Like that above.

Let music swell the breeze
And ring from all the trees
  Sweet Freedom's song!
Let mortal tongues awake,
Let all that breathe partake,
Let rocks their silence break,
  The sound prolong.

Our fathers' God, to thee,
Author of Liberty!
  To Thee we sing:
Long may our land be bright
With freedom's holy light,
Protect us by Thy might,
  Great God, our king!

Peace follows where it finds the Old Thirteen, the nucleus around which the other stars have gathered in their glory.

—*Letitia Green Stevenson,*
Honorary Vice President General National Society, Daughters of the
American Revolution.

The Old Thirteen

A PATRIOTIC SONG

DEDICATED TO THE

SONS, DAUGHTERS AND CHILDREN OF THE

AMERICAN REVOLUTION

1. 'Flag of the free, we hail thee with pride, Float thou in free-dom o'er all the land wide; Em-blem of pow'r wher-e'er thou art seen, Yet still we are true to The Old Thir-teen. Our fa-thers who fought a free

2. We'll work for thy glo-ry for-ev-er and aye, We'll cel-e-brate ev-er that dear-ly bought day, Thy folds float-ing o'er us in tri-umph were seen, So val-iant-ly won by The Old Thir-teen We'll ral-ly a-round thee from

coun - try to make, Who suf - fered and died for sweet lib - er - ty's sake, What
near and from far, Our stand - ard for - ev - er in peace or in war, All

Cres.

joy had been theirs had they on - ly fore-seen How vast we should grow from The
na - tions sa - lute thee, thy stars might-y sheen. Full splen - dor thou art of The

Old Thir - teen - For - ty - five stars now shine in thy blue,
Old Thir - teen. Then hail we our em-blem, each daugh-ter and son,

Cres.

For - ty five states to thee will be true— As he - roes of old keep their
Hon - or the vic - t'ry ,thy fair folds have won; Tho' mul - ti - plied stars float in

Dim.

mem - o - ry green, Who marched with the flag of The Old Thir - teen.
free - dom se - rene. En - shrined in our hearts is The Old Thir - teen.

WORDS BY Cornelia Copeland Lewis MUSIC BY Harriet Hayden Hayes

STARS ON THE FLAG.

The Home Magazine contains the following beautiful suggestion regarding the placing of the stars on the flag:

Number 1 is the field of our first stars and stripes made by Betsy Ross.

Number 2 represents that field of flag of 1814 which inspired the "Star Spangled Banner."

Number 3 the field of 1818 designed by Capt. S. C. Reid.

Number 4, field of our present flag.

Although there is no law saying who shall arrange the stars on our flag, or how they shall be arranged, it is customary for the changes to be made in the war department when new states have been admitted to the Union.

1   *2*   *3*   *4*

The incongruous variations in figures A, B, C, which are reproductions of unions taken from new flags, made by different manufacturers, would not exist if there was a law fixing the arrangement of the stars.

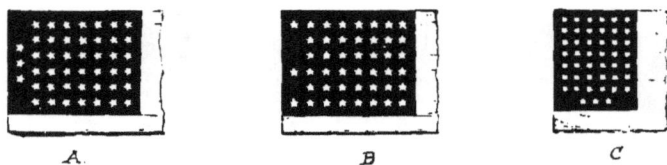

A.   *B*   *C*

It is believed by many that the stars on our flag should be arranged into a permanent and symmetrical form, fixed by law, instead of the present changeable and uncertain form, which is subject in a great measure, to the caprice or convenience of the flag maker. It is not generally known that among the many flags in use in our country to-day, there is an utter lack of uniformity in the arrangement of the stars.

In the selection of a form, three different things should be considered—its historical significance, symmetry, and adaptability. The stars should be so arranged that it will not be necessary to make any noticeable change when new ones are added. The stars should always remain equal in size, representing the equality of the states.

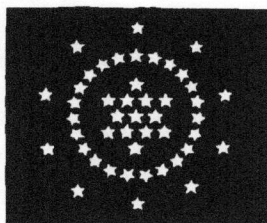

In the form which is submitted, No. 8, with the group of thirteen stars in the center, representing the thirteen original states, they are arranged in exactly the same form as they appear on the great seal of the United States. The circle containing twenty-three stars, represents the states which were admitted to the Union up to the close of the civil war. These two features are symbolic of the two great events in the nation's history—the one which brought our flag into existence, and the other which made its life permanent by welding the sisterhood of states into a perfect and indestructible union. The circle is also symbolic of unity, peace, and preservation.

3

The outside circle of nine stars, represents the states which have been added to the Union since the civil war. New stars can be added to this circle without changing the symmetry of the arrangement, as will be seen by reference to the illustration. As this circle will always remain an open one, there will always be room for one more star, and it is thus significant of progression.

One great advantage in this form is, that it is suggestive of a constellation, and thus carries out, as far as practicable, the idea of the framers of the resolution of 1777 in establishing the flag.

John F. Earhart is the author of the above description of the different forms of flags.

THE LIBERTY CAP.

The historians who have searched the archives of ancient and medieval times tell us that this has been a symbol of liberty since the Phrygians made the conquest of the eastern part of Asia Minor.

After the conquest they stamped it on their coins, and to distinguish themselves from the primitive peoples they used the liberty cap as a head dress. The Romans used a small red cap called a "pileus," which they placed on the head of a slave in making him free, and when Caesar was murdered a Phrygian cap was carried through the streets of Rome proclaiming the liberty of the people. The liberty cap of the English is blue with a white border.

It remained for the United States to adopt the British cap, adding to it the crescent of thirteen stars. Generals Lee and Schuyler, with the Philadelphia Light Horse troop, adopted it in 1775. This is the famous troop that escorted Washington to New York.

It is most familiar to us as seen on our coins, on which it was first used after the Revolution as a symbol of freedom.

Edward Everett Hale, in one of his impressive orations, says: "The starry banner speaks for itself; its mute eloquence needs no aid to interpret its significance. Fidelity to the Union blazes from its stars; allegiance to the government beneath which we live is wrapped in its folds."

The Stars and Stripes was officially first unfolded over Ft. Schuyler, a military port in New York state, now the city of Rome, Oneida county. It was first saluted on the sea by a foreign power, when floating from the masthead of the Ranger, Capt. Paul Jones commanding, at Quiberon Bay, France, February 14, 1778. The salute was given by Admiral La Motte, representing the French government.

The first vessel over which the Union flag floated was the ship Ranger, built at Portsmouth, New Hampshire, whose gallant commander was the famous Paul Jones.

Its first trip around the world was on the ship Columbia, which left Boston September 30, 1787, commanded by Captains Kendrick and Gray. It was three years then in circling the globe. To-day it waves in every clime, on every sea.

It is pleasing to note how Franklin, when minister to France, secured the ship Doria from the French and gave to Paul Jones the command, who immediately renamed the old ship "Bon homme Richard," in honor of Franklin.

ORIGIN OF "OLD GLORY."

The term Old Glory is said to have been originated by an old sailor—Stephen Driver.

While upon the seas he performed an act of bravery for which he was rewarded by the gift of an American flag, whereupon he pledged its givers to always defend it faithfully.

At the outbreak of the civil war he was living in Nashville, Tenn.

In order to keep the flag safely he concealed it in a bed-quilt under which he slept. To the enemies of the Union he declared that Old Glory would yet float from the staff of the Tennessee state house, and sure enough when Nashville fell into the hands of Gen. Buell he secured the flag from its hiding place and hoisted it to a more fitting position on the state house—thus his nick-name for it became popular.

JOHN JAY AT MOUNT KISCO, JULY 4, 1861.

He said, "Swear anew and teach the oath to our children, that with God's help the American Republic shall stand un-moved though all the powers of piracy and European jealousy should combine to overthrow it.   That we shall have in the fu-ture as we have had in the past, one country, one constitution, one destiny; and that when we shall have passed from earth, and the acts of to-day shall be matters of history, and the dark power which sought our overthrow shall have been overthrown, our sons may gather strength from our example in every con-test with despotism that time may have in store to try their virtue, and that they may rally under the Stars and Stripes with our old time war cry,

" 'Liberty and Union, now and forever, one and inseparable.' "

UNCLE SAM.

This term originated at the time of our war with England in 1812.   Provisions were purchased at Troy, N. Y., and the agent was Elbert Anderson, the work being superintended by Ebe-nezer and Samuel Wilson, the packages being marked E. A. U. S.   Samuel Wilson was known all over as Uncle Sam and he was often joked about his amount of provisions, then the newspapers took it up and the term Uncle Sam came into general use and is typical of our increasing national prosperity. Quite recently a portrait of an actual personage whose features are identical with those made familiar by caricatures of Uncle Sam, was found in possession of a family near Toledo, Ohio. The portrait was painted about 1818, but nothing is known of the shrewd, kindly old man represented. His face was undoubtedly the origin of the accepted caricature

BROTHER JONATHAN.

Jonathan Trumbull, governor of Connecticut, was a warm friend of General Washington, who had great confidence in his judgment.

When in need of ammunition and the question arose as to where they could get the necessary means for defense Washington said: "We will consult Brother Jonathan."

After that whenever they needed help the expression became a common one and naturally came to mean the United States Government.

THE AMERICAN EAGLE.

Our bald headed eagle, so called because the feathers on the top of the head are white, was named the Washington eagle by Audubon. Like Washington it was brave and fearless, and as his name and greatness is known the world over, so the greatest of birds can soar to the heights beyond all others.

In 1785 it became the emblem of the United States.

It is used on the tips of flag staffs, on coins, on the United States seals, and on the shield of liberty.

BANNERS AND STANDARDS.

It is not generally known that the tassels which are pendent customarily from the upper part of banners and standards, and the fringe which surrounds them are relics of the practice of observing sacred emblems. They originated in pagan devices and the garments of priests and were consecrated to specific forms of worship.

Sacred history is full of instances of the consecration of tassels and peculiar fringes to special sacerdotal uses. Blue was early the emblem of purity and innocence and that fact accounts for the predominance of that color in the ecclesiastical badges of these early times. When the use of the tassels passed into profane customs, they were used as ornaments for national standards and for royal girdles, and it was not infrequent that they were first blessed by the priests. It has followed naturally that this use has continued up to the present time, although now it is retained probably because of the artistic effect of the swinging pendants.

THE LINCOLN FLAG.

Presented by the French People.

The flag in the White House which formerly hung in the center of the largest window in the east room, has a unique history.

It is woven of silk in one piece without a seam. There are gold stars in the field and among them are seen the words in French, "Popular subscription to the Republic of the United States, offered in memory of Abraham Lincoln. Lyons, 1865."

STATE FLAGS.

As the colonies had their flags of different kinds so the states one by one adopted special flags and nearly all the states of the Union now have a state flag or regimental color. In some states this emblem is established by law, in other states by the

military department or the governor. There are a few states
in which this special flag is covered with particular devices
chosen by the caprice of the donor or the officials by whom the
flag was authorized, but in all these cases, the state arms form
a part of the emblazonment. There is a general feeling, however, that these special states flags should have no legal recog-
nition, and that the only flag to be thus recognized should be
the Stars and Stripes.

ORIGIN OF THE FLAG OF TRUCE.

It is interesting to know how and why the little white flag
which is always looked upon with breathless interest in the
emergencies that call it forth, first came to be used.

When carried by the lone soldier on horse or on foot between the armies it has a significance that is always respected,
and on the sea the hoisting of this flag at the ship's mast or
the carrying of the flag of white by boat to the enemy stops
the firing of the guns. The custom originated in the church in
the tenth or eleventh century.

Curiously enough while it is the only flag that is to-day used
by all nations of the earth alike, no regularly made flag of
truce is found in the flag lockers of nations. It is improvised
when the emergency arises for its use. In the late war with
Spain, such flags of truce as were used were made of blank-
ets, sheets, table cloths. It is a flag that commands the enemy's respect. An account of the origin of the flag of truce
lately published, is as follows:

"La peace et la treve de Dieu" (The peace and the truce of
God) was an agreement between the turbulent barons and the
church, as severe injury and loss was most frequently the result of the private warfares which constantly raged.

To protect itself, but more especially to preserve justice and
moral order, the church established a system which has exer-
cised a beneficent influence down to this day.

The agreement stipulated a cessation of hostilities on certain festivities and saint's days, and from Saturday to Monday. The barons and warrior class pledged during the time of war to extend full protection to women, pilgrims, priests, monks, travelers, merchants and agriculturists; to abstain from the destruction or injury of farm implements, the burning of crops, and the killing of live stock of the peasants. Penalties in violation of this agreement comprised money fines, bafflings, banishment, and excommunication.

Originating in the south of France this system was soon adopted through the whole of France, Italy, Spain, Germany, and England, and in 1095 Pope Urban II. proclaimed its universal extension throughout Christendom.

In time the Crown assumed this protective power, and the phrase was changed to "La paix et la treve du Roi," or "The peace and truce of the king." The republics recognized the time-honored institution, and the simple unfolding of a white cloth will instantly cause a cessation of hostilities. The adoption of a white emblem appears to be lost in tradition, as authorities do not reveal it. Doubtless it is similar, or may have arisen through a belief in the white Samite which shielded the Holy Grail from the gaze of unbelievers. Emblematic of purity, associated with the mythical knights of the Round Table, and used in the Crusades, it is probable that this sacred truce flag may have originated from the Samite of the Holy Grail.

At the present time, if presented during an engagement firing is not required to cease; nor, if the bearer be killed or wounded, is there ground for complaint. The truce emblem can be retained if admitted, during an engagement. Penalties are incurred if the truce emblem be wrongfully used, the severest being the ignominious death of a spy.

The following was written at the tomb of Washington in 1833 by Dr. Andrew Reed, English philanthropist:

WASHINGTON.

The Brave   The Wise.   The Good.

Supreme in War, in Council and in Peace.

WASHINGTON.

Valiant	Discreet	Confident
without	without	without
Ambition.	Fear.	Presumption.

WASHINGTON.

In Disaster Calm.   In Success Moderate.   In All Himself.

WASHINGTON.

The Hero.   The Patriot.   The Christian.

The Father of Nations, the friend of Mankind
who
When he had won all renounced all
and sought
In the Bosom of his family and of Nature
Retirement
And in the hope of Religion
Immortality.

JANE CLAYPOOLE CANBY,
Fourth Daughter of Betsy Ross.

SKETCH OF BETSY ROSS AND HER HUSBANDS.

Elizabeth Griscom, a daughter of Samuel and Rebecka (James) Griscom of Philadelphia, was born January 1, 1752. They were "Friends" and the young Elizabeth grew into a most charming, bright and beautiful girl of prepossessing manners and plain and quiet tastes.

Her father was a noted builder and assisted in the erection of the state house, now Independence Hall. His house, shop and a very large garden were on Arch street, between 3d and 4th streets.

Elizabeth, or Betsy, as she was fondly called, was the seventh daughter. Her birthday was the first day under the new Gregorian calendar.

It was frequently said by the family that "she was born the first day of the month, the first day of the year, the first day of the new style." She was well trained by her mother, became very expert with her needle and was very fond of embroidery.

Among her many admirers was John Ross, son of Æneas Ross, assistant rector of Christ Episcopal Church. The young man was a nephew of the Hon. George Ross, delegate to Congress, one of the signers of the Declaration of Independence.

In December, 1773, at the age of twenty-one years, Elizabeth married John Ross, an estimable young man. He was an Episcopalian, and in consequence of her marrying out of meeting, she was disowned by the Friends.

The first husband of Betsy Ross was of distinguished ancestry. The Hon. George Ross, of New Castle, Delaware, had by his first wife, two sons: John, who died May 5th, 1776; and Rev. Æneas, born Sept. 9th. 1716, who was father of John Ross (husband of Betsy Ross).

By his second wife he had Hon. George Ross, signer of Declaration of Independence, born 1730, died 1780; also one daughter, Gertrude, who married George Read, also a signer of the Declaration of Independence; also a son, Jacob, a physician.

The Hon. George Ross was a noted lawyer, and a resident of Lancaster. He was a brave soldier and a man of ability.

John Ross was an apprentice with a man named Webster, an upholsterer on Chestnut street. It was with him that John and afterwards Betsy, learned the trade before they "ran off" to be married.

They then set up business for themselves, first on Chestnut street and afterwards moved to the little house on Arch street, which was a simple building when first occupied by them. It was built some time after 1752, notwithstanding romantic stories to the contrary. The first room was utilized as a shop; the store front not having been added until about 1858.

It was in this house that the flag was made later on.

In 1775 John Ross was injured while guarding military stores on the wharf, from the effects of which he died at this house in January, 1776. He was buried in Christ Churchyard, 5th and Arch streets. He left no children.

Mrs. Ross continued the upholstery business and the manufacture of flags.

Betsy Ross married for her second husband, at Old Swedes Church, Philadelphia, Captain Joseph Ashburn, June 15, 1777, and to them were born two daughters:

Jillah, born September 15th, 1779. Died young.

Eliza, born February 25th, 1781. Who married Capt. Isaack Silliman, May 29th, 1799. After Capt. Silliman's death in the army, his wife Eliza lived with her mother, Betsy Ross, until her death in 1836.

To them were born four children:

Joseph Ashburn; Emilia; Jane; Willys.

Emilia left one daughter, Mrs. Mary Sidney Garrett, a widow and childless. She is the only living descendant of the second marriage.

Joseph Ashburn was taken prisoner by the British on the sea, and with the other soldiers was taken to England where he died in Mill Prison, March 3d, 1782. The prisoners were all given an opportunity to enter the British service, and on their refusal were thrown into prison. John Claypole, a comrade, and also a prisoner of war, nursed and cared for Ashburn until he died. He brought home to his widow, on his release, the diary of Ashburn, together with messages to his wife, with whom he fell in love and afterward married.

John Claypoole, son of William and Elizabeth Claypoole, of Philadelphia, was married to Elizabeth Ashburn (Betsy Ross) the 8th of May, 1783, at Christ Church. His ancestor was James Claypoole, who came to America as the friend of William Penn; and from whom all the Claypooles mentioned are descended. He was a brother of Sir John Claypoole, who married Elizabeth, daughter of Oliver Cromwell.

The children of John and Elizabeth Claypoole were: Clarissa Sidney, born April 3, 1785, 9 a. m.; Susanna, born November 15, 1786, 4 p. m.; Rachel, born February 1, 1789, 7 p. m.; Jane, born November 13, 1793, 7 p. m.; Harriet, born December 20, 1795, 5 a. m., died October 8, 1796.

There is an old Bible over a hundred years old, which has a record of all these births and those of the Ashburn daughters; and of the deaths in the handwriting of John Claypoole. It was "The legacy of Sarah Hallowell to her niece, Elizabeth Claypoole," that is, Betsy Ross.

John Claypoole was wounded in the battle of Germantown which, with imprisonment and the hardships of war, so impaired his health that he never regained it. So it may be truthfully said that the lives of her three husbands were sacrificed to their country, and her experience in these very important events in her life is certainly heroic. John Claypoole died August 3, 1817.

Betsy Ross attended Christ Church, Philadelphia, with her first husband and after his death continued in attendance until the Free Quaker Society was organized in 1793. The pew in which she sat was quite near one occupied by Gen. Washington, and is marked by a brass plate bearing these words:

"In this pew worshipped Betsey Ross, who made the first flag."

All Friends who took part in the Revolution were disowned by "The Society of Friends." After the war, they organized a society of "Free Quakers" often called "Fighting Quakers."

As the time went by, nearly all were taken back into the original "Society of Friends," but Clarissa Wilson and John Price Wetherell, of Philadelphia, were the last of the Free Quakers. They used to attend the little meeting house at 5th and Arch streets until there were just the two of them. In the fall of 1830 they decided it was unwise to have the little meeting house heated for them, so after that Clarissa Wilson attended the Orange street meeting house, but was never again received into the original society. She did not wish to be. She died a Free Quaker. Betsy Ross, her mother, lived to be 84 years old and died in 1836. The following are from the original autographs of Betsy Ross and her husband:

Elizabeth Claypoole

John Claypoole

CHILDREN OF JOHN AND BETSY ROSS CLAYPOOLE.

Clarissa Sidney (Wilson)	Elizabeth Griscom } twins	married	James Campion
	Sophia }	"	Charles Hildebrandt
	Aquila Bolton	married	Sarah Ghriskey
	Clarissa Sidney	"	James Hanna
	Susan	"	Abram Sellers
	Rachel	"	Jacob Wilson Albright

Susanna (Satterthwaite)	James	bachelor	
	Edwin	married	Martha Hallowell
	Abel	"	Mary Burton
	Sidney	"	Cyrus Kinsey
	Mary	not married	
	Susan	married	David Newport } This couple still living in 1898 at Willow Grove, Philadelphia

Rachel (1st, Edward Jones; 2nd, John Fletcher)	Margaretta	married	—— Elliot
	Mary	"	Arthur Wigert
	Daniel	not married; died at 21 yrs. of age	

Jane (Canby)	Catharine	married	Lloyd Balderston
	Elizabeth	unmarried	
	Charles	married	Susanna Kirk
	John	"	Elizabeth Boustead
	William	"	Louise Prescott
	Caleb	"	Mary Preswick
	George	"	Matilda Goodwin
	Jane	"	Abel Hopkins } Nephew of Johns Hopkins
	Mary	"	Robert Culin

THE OLD KEY MANSION.

The old Key mansion is one of the historic places that still remains on the banks of the Potomac in Georgetown, to remind us that here lived Francis Scott Key, the author of the national hymn "The Star Spangled Banner." In unveiling to him the monument which had been erected at Fredericksburg, Maryland, during the past summer (1898), the Hon. Murat Halsted paid an eloquent tribute to this poet, who crystallized the best thought of the American people in giving to them "The Star Spangled Banner." "O'er the land of the free and the home of the brave," this flag still waves. Freedom to-day has a broader meaning than in the days of 1814. Slavery has been abolished and freedom has spread her wings o'er all the land. The history of the writing of this beautiful song can be told in a few words. It was an inspiration. The British had captured a friend of Francis Scott Key, Dr. Beans, and when Key heard of it, he called upon President Madison, who furnished him with a vessel to go to the British Admiral Cockburn's ship, to endeavor to secure his release. General Ross, of the British army, agreed to release him, but insisted upon Key's remaining on the admiral's ship until after the bombardment of Fort McHenry, which was then taking place. Key was intensely anxious and in the early morning, he looked across to the fort and saw that "the flag was still there." It is said that he then wrote a sketch of the "Star Spangled Banner" on the back of a letter. The burning of the capitol and of the White House a few days previous by them are well known matters of history. A few days after, the British fleet sailed for Baltimore, where they were gallantly repulsed with the loss of their commander, General Ross. The fleet in passing Mount Vernon, lowered their flags out of respect to the memory of the immortal Washington, whose remains are here entombed.

4

Key was born in Frederick county, Maryland, August 1, 1779. He graduated at St. John's College, Annapolis, Maryland.

_____

THE STAR-SPANGLED BANNER.

Oh, say, can you see by the dawn's early light
   What so proudly we hailed at the twilight's last gleaming,
Whose broad stripes and bright stars through the perilous fight,
   O'er the ramparts we watched were so gallantly streaming;
And the rocket's red glare, the bombs bursting in air,
Gave proof through the night that our flag was still there!
Oh, say, does that star-spangled banner yet wave
O'er the land of the free and the home of the brave.

On that shore, dimly seen through the mist of the deep,
   Where the foe's haughty host in dread silence reposes,
What is that which the breeze o'er the tow'ring steep,
   As it fitfully blows, now conceals, now discloses?
Now it catches the gleam of the morning's first beam
In full glory reflected now shines on the stream.
'Tis the star-spangled banner, oh, long may it wave
O'er the land of the free and the home of the brave.

And where is that foe which so vauntingly swore,
   That the havoc of war and the battle's confusion,
A home and a country should leave us no more?
   Their blood has washed out their foul footsteps' pollution;
No refuge could save the hireling and slave
From the terror or flight or the gloom of the grave.
And the star-spangled banner in triumph doth wave
O'er the land of the free and the home of the brave!

Oh, thus be it ever, when freemen shall stand,
   Between their loved homes and the war's desolation;
Blest with vict'ry and peace, may the heaven-rescued land
   Praise the Power that hath made and preserved us a nation.
Then conquer we must when our cause it is just,
And this be our motto, "In God is our trust";
And the star-spangled banner in triumph shall wave
O'er the land of the free and the home of the brave.
                    —Francis Scott Key, 1814.

COPYRIGHT 1888. BY ADDIE G. WEAVER.

INVOCATION TO THE FLAG.
Dedicated to the D. A. R.'s.

Our own dear flag, the stripes and stars,
    In peace like "bird of promise" flying,
When War's dread battles fiercely wage,
    All tyranny and wrong defying.

Legions beneath its beckoning folds,
    Start at the sound of bugle calling.
Eager to lift oppression's yoke,
    From fainting brothers, bravely falling.

Lead on, dear flag, our heroes true,
    O'er mountain pass and wild savanna.
Till victories by their prowess won,
    Ring a new nation's glad hozanna.

Float o'er them where they bravely stand,
    The bursting shell and cannon daring,
And glory wreathe their chaplets fair,
    Who fall, another's burden sharing.

Wave proudly on, where hastening ships
    Sweep the white wave, like tempest flying.
Give freedom to the toiling slave,
    Give life to Cuba's children dying.

Shine on, bright stars, glad folds unroll
    O'er far-off islands care beseeching.
Lighten old Afric's age of night,
    Give aid to Asia's millions reaching.

On wings of dawn, where Orient smiles,
    To gates of sunset, ocean laving,
Bear light and hope, while earth shall hail,
    Our flag, for right and freedom waving.

June 14th, 1898.
                              CARRIE P. GUTHRIE.

UNFURL THE FLAG.

By Rev. Artemas Jean Haynes, Pastor Plymouth Church, Chicago.

Unfurl the flag! the flag of freedom's birth—
  The stainless banner of our loyal host;
Unfurl the flag! proclaim to all the earth
  That war for conquest is not Freedom's boast.
Shake out the crimson folds in God's great strife—
Our country's pledge to liberty and life.

Unfurl the flag! stand forth in Christ's own name—
  For God's dread day of Judgment is at hand;
Unfurl the flag! and smite with sudden shame,
  Relentless tyrants from our sisterland.
Each waving fold of white, each star shall bear
Our love to those whose griefs we seek to share.

Unfurl the flag! we battle not for gain—
  We march as those who march to right a wrong;
Unfurl the flag! not to avenge the slain,
  Unfurl it for the weak who trust the strong:
Fling out the blue! our battle flag unfurled—
Warfare for love, and freedom for the world.

Unfurl the flag! red, white and blue wave high—
  Wave on to battle every loyal son;
Unfurl the flag! hear Thou, O God, our cry—
  Blaze Thou the way until our task be done;
Until the night falls on the hosts of wrong,
And morning breaks to Freedom's triumph song.

THE AMERICAN FLAG.
By Joseph Rodman Drake.

When Freedom from her mountain height
  Unfurled her standard to the air,
She tore the azure robe of night.
  And set the stars of glory there;
She mingled with its glorious dyes
The milky baldric of the skies.
And striped its pure celestial white
With streakings of the morning's light;
Then from his mansion in the sun
She called her eagle-bearer down,
And gave into his mighty hand
The symbol of her chosen land.

Majestic monarch of the cloud!
  Who rear'st aloft thy regal form,
To hear the tempest-trumpings loud,
And see the lightning lances driven.
  When strive the warriors of the storm,
And rolls the thunder drum of heaven—
Child of the sun! to thee 'tis given
To guard the banner of the free,
To hover in the sulphur'us smoke,
To ward away the battle-stroke,
And bid its blendings shine afar,
Like rainbows on the cloud of war,
The harbingers of victory.

Flag of the brave, thy folds shall fly
The sign of hope and triumph high,
When speaks the signal trumpet tone,
And the long line comes gleaming on;
And yet the life blood, warm and wet,
Has dimmed the glistening bayonet,

Each soldier's eye shall brightly turn,
To where thy sky-born glories burn;
And, as his springing steps advance,
Catch war and vengeance from the glance;
And when the cannon-mouthings loud,
Heave in wild wreaths the battle-shroud,
And gory sabers rise and fall,
Like shoots of flame on midnight's pall,
There shall thy meteor glances glow,
    And cowering foes shall sink beneath
Each gallant arm that strikes below
    That lovely messenger of death.

Flag of the seas, on ocean wave,
Thy stars shall glitter o'er the brave;
When Death, careering on the gale,
Sweeps darkly round the bellied sail,
And frighted waves, rush wildly back,
Before the broadside's reeling rack,
Each dying wanderer of the sea
Shall look at once to heaven and thee,
And smile to see thy splendors fly
In triumph o'er his closing eye.

Flag of the free heart's hope and home,
    By angel hands to valor given!
Thy stars have lit the welkin dome,
    And all thy hues were born in heaven.
Forever float that standard sheet!
    Where breathes the foe but falls before us,
With Freedom's soil beneath our feet,
    And Freedom's banner streaming o'er us!

Fitz Greene Halleck wrote the last four lines of this poem.

BATTLE HYMN OF THE REPUBLIC.

This beautiful song, which is set to the tune of "John Brown," was written by Julia Ward Howe in 1861 just after her escape from a rebel raid when witnessing, with friends, a review of troops near Washington. In her dreams she was inspired by the beautiful thoughts and she immediately arose, and hastily noted them down.

It is considered one of the grandest battle hymns of the Republic and has been a favorite with several of our presidents.

BATTLE HYMN OF THE REPUBLIC.

Mine eyes have seen the glory of the coming of the Lord!
He is trampling out the vintage where the grapes of wrath are stored;
He hath loosed the fateful lightning of His terrible, swift sword,
    His truth is marching on!

I have seen Him in the watchfires of a hundred circling camps,
They have builded Him an altar in the evening dews and damps;
I have read His righteous sentence by the dim and flaring lamps,
    His day is marching on!

There read a fiery gospel writ in burnished rows of steel;
"As ye deal with my contemners, so with you my grace shall deal!
Let the Hero, born of woman, crush the serpent with His heel,
    Since God is marching on!

He has sounded forth the trumpet that shall never call retreat!
He is sifting out the hearts of men before His judgment seat;
Oh, be swift, my soul, to answer Him! be jubilant, my feet,
    Our God is marching on.

In the beauty of the lilies Christ was born across the sea,
With a glory in His bosom that transfigures you and me;
As He died to make men holy, let us die to make men free.
    While God is marching on.

CHICKAMAUGA.

This beautiful poem was written during the late war with Spain, and is inserted here, as entwined among the lines there is a sentiment that appeals to the hearts of the whole people.

CHICKAMAUGA.

They are camped on Chickamauga!
　Once again the white tents gleam
On that field where vanished heroes
　Sleep the sleep that knows no dream.
There are shadows all about them
　Of the ghostly troops to-day,
But they light the common campfire—
　Those who wore the blue and gray.

Where the pines of Georgia tower,
　Where the mountains kiss the sky,
On their arms the nation's warriors
　Wait to hear the battle cry.
Wait together, friends and brothers,
　And the heroes 'neath their feet
Sleep the long and dreamless slumber
　Where the flowers are blooming sweet.

Sentries, pause, yon shadow challenge!
　Rock-ribbed Thomas goes that way—
He who fought the foes unyielding
　In that awful battle fray.
Yonder pass the shades of heroes,
　And they follow where Bragg leads
Through the meadows and the river,
　But no ghost the sentry heeds.

Field of fame, a patriot army
  Treads thy sacred sod to-day!
And they'll fight a common foeman,
  Those who wore the blue and gray,
And they'll fight for common country,
  And they'll charge to victory
'Neath the folds of one brave banner—
  Starry banner of the free!

They are camped on Chickamauga,
  Where the green tents of the dead
Turn the soil into a glory
  Where a nation's heart once bled;
But they're clasping hands together
  On this storied field of strife—
Brothers brave who meet to battle
  In the freedom-war of life!

                              —Baltimore News.

THE BON HOMME RICHARD FLAG.

This historic old flag, also known as the Paul Jones Flag, composed of thirteen bars and but twelve stars, was unfurled by him and borne on the Bon Homme Richard September 23, 1776, during the action with the British frigate, the "Serapis," and is probably the first flag bearing the stars and stripes ever hoisted over an American vessel of war, and also the first ever saluted by a foreign naval power.

This flag has been in the family of Mrs. H. R. P. Stafford, of Cottage City, Martha's Vineyard, since 1784, and bequeathed by her to the National Museum at Washington.

But it must be remembered that Washington adopted the flag made by Betsy Ross five months previous to this.

"THE OLD THIRTEEN."
A Leaf from Illinois' History.

In the little city of Shawneetown which is next in age to Kaskaskia, and consequently the second oldest town in the State, there reposes a relic of rare value, a genuine flag of Colonial days. It was found in the attic of the "Posey" building and is supposed to have been placed there by General Posey, who served under Washington in the Revolutionary war. The flag is now owned by Mr. Robinson, an eminent scientist, who for a life-time has taken pains to collect and preserve many valuable things for Illinois' posterity to see, especially rare Indian curios excavated from in and around Shawneetown, which site was once the pottery of the Shawanee Indians.

The old flag is in rather a good state of preservation although faded and marred. Its thirteen stars are arranged similar to those on "Paul Jones' flag"—in bars, but not horizontal. The rows of stars are placed diagonally and consist of one, three, five, three and one, which leaves a star in each corner and five forming the center diagonal.   Illinois' "Old Thirteen" has been framed and covered with glass to preserve it from the ravages of Time and to save it for the eyes of the children of coming generations.

COLUMBIA, THE GEM OF THE OCEAN.

Columbia, the gem of the ocean,
　The home of the brave and the free;
The shrine of each patriot's devotion,
　A world offers homage to thee;
Thy mandates make heroes assemble;
　When liberty's form stands in view;
Thy banners make tyranny tremble,
　When borne by the red, white and blue.

Three cheers for the red, white and blue,
Three cheers for the red, white and blue,
Thy mandates make tyranny tremble,
When borne by the red, white and blue.

This song sometimes goes by the title of The Red, White and Blue.   It was written and composed by David T. Shaw in 1843; later on, however, it was rearranged by Thomas à Becket, Esq., an Englishman.

HAIL COLUMBIA.

This was written by Hon. Joseph Hopkinson, of Philadelphia, at the request of a young friend—a theatrical singer whose appeal was for a patriotic song suitable for the times. England and France were quarreling and this country was necessarily a good deal agitated.

It was set to the music called The President's March, which was composed by Philip Roth, a German, for Gen. Washington's inauguration in the City Hall in New York. A great many people were for standing by our ally, France, but Gen. Washington insisted on strict neutrality; thus the song was required to voice this sentiment. It appealed at once to both parties and charmed every one who heard it—was sung night after night, audiences joining in the chorus.

"Hail Columbia, happy land!
Hail, ye heroes, heaven-born band;
Who fought and bled in freedom's cause.
Who fought and bled in freedom's cause.
And when the storm of war was gone
Enjoyed the peace your valor won;
Let independence be our boast,
Ever mindful what it cost,
Ever grateful for the prize,
Let the altar reach the skies.

Chorus—Firm, united let us be,
        Rallying round our liberty;
        As a band of brothers joined,
        Peace and safety shall we find.

"Immortal patriot, rise once more,
 Defend your rights, defend your shore;
 Let no rude foe with impious hand,
 Let no rude foe with impious hand,
 Invade the shrine where sacred lies
 Of toil and blood the well-earned prize.
 While offering peace, sincere and just,
 In heaven we place our manly trust
 That truth and justice shall prevail.
 And every scheme of bondage fail."—Cho.

DIXIE.

Southrons, hear your country call you!
Up, lest worse than death befall you!
    To arms! to arms! to arms in Dixie.
Lo, all the beaconfires are lighted,
Let all hearts be now united,
    To arms! to arms! to arms in Dixie.

    Chorus—
Advance the flag of Dixie!
Hurrah! Hurrah!
For Dixie's land we'll take our stand,
To live or die for Dixie!
To arms! To arms!
And conquer peace for Dixie!
To arms! To arms!
And conquer peace for Dixie!

Hear the northern thunders mutter!
Northern flags in south wind flutter!
    To arms! to arms! to arms in Dixie!
Send them back your fierce defiance,
Stamp upon the cursed alliance;
    To arms! to arms! to arms in Dixie!

Fear no danger, shun no labor,
Lift up rifle, pike and saber!
   To arms! to arms! to arms in Dixie!
Shoulder pressing close to shoulder,
Let the odds make each heart bolder;
   To arms! to arms! to arms in Dixie!

Swear upon your country's altar
Never to give up or falter;
   To arms! to arms! to arms in Dixie!
Till the spoilers are defeated,
Till the Lord's work is completed,
   To arms! to arms! to arms in Dixie!

If the loved ones weep in sadness,
Victory soon shall bring them gladness,
   To arms! to arms! to arms in Dixie!
Exultant pride soon banish sorrow;
Smiles chase tears away to-morrow;
   To arms! to arms! to arms in Dixie!

   Chorus—
Advance the flag of Dixie!
Hurrah! Hurrah!
In Dixie's land we'll take our stand,
To live or die for Dixie!
To arms! To arms!
And conquer peace for Dixie!
To arms! To arms!
And conquer peace for Dixie!
              —[Albert Pike.

TERRITORIAL EXPANSION.

Washington took the oath of office as first President of the United States on the steps of Federal Hall in Wall street, New York city, April 30, 1789, and for a short time the seat of government was here before being changed to Philadelphia.

The history of how Alexander Hamilton, the great Secretary of the Treasury under Washington, made the trade with Jefferson whereby the present site of the capital was selected is interesting, as showing that Hamilton, while constructing a powerful centralized government with skill and ability, as even Jefferson's biographer admits, cared little about the location of the capital itself. The Southern States wanted it on the Potomac; the Middle and Eastern States wished it to be further north. Hamilton wanted the government to assume the State debts, brought about by the war. Jefferson and his party were opposed to it. Hamilton finally secured the support of Jefferson and his friends in Congress in support of the assumption, while he delivered to the Jefferson party the location of the capital at Washington. In after years this was a source of great discomfort to Jefferson, he claiming to have been duped by Hamilton.

ACQUISITION OF TERRITORY.
LOUISIANA.

In 1800 Napoleon forced Spain to cede Louisiana back to France, after thirty-seven years of ownership. The idea of La-Salle, who had looked forward to establishing here a new France, was long since forgotten, but Napoleon, now in the zenith of his power, formed the brilliant plan of colonizing this great country from the Mississippi to the Rockies and from the Gulf to the British possessions in the North, thereby hemming in the United States. Napoleon tried to subdue the Island of San Domingo, with the idea of using it as an outside base of supplies, but his troops were terribly slaughtered by the natives, and the army that he intended to send to Louisiana never came. About this time Napoleon was busy looking after England, and as after events proved needed all of his troops at home. He succeeded, however, in creating great alarm in America. The settlers west of the Alleghenies were especially disturbed. The Mississippi was practically closed for navigation, as the Spaniards, who held possession of New Orleans, would not allow them to bring their products down the river and reship, as had long been the custom.

President Jefferson appointed James Monroe and Livingston, then our minister at Paris, to call on Napoleon, and, if possible, purchase West Florida and New Orleans, the amount to be paid not to exceed $3,000,000.

Napoleon was very much in need of money to conduct his war against England, and his disastrous attempt to subdue the natives of San Domingo probably made him decide to offer the whole of Louisiana, which he did for $15,000,000. This great purchase was consummated by Monroe in 1803. This was the greatest act of Jefferson's administration, but the people bitterly opposed it, claiming that we had no use for the additional territory. Napoleon said that in selling Louisiana to the United States "he had placed a thorn where England would some day feel it." The acquisition of Louisiana more than doubled the area of the United States, which was 827,844 square miles, increasing it to 1,999,775 square miles. It constitutes about ten of our largest States to-day.

FLORIDA.

This State, with all its old traditions, has seen many vicissitudes. It belonged to Spain from 1565 until 1763, nearly one hundred years, when Great Britain traded Cuba for it. In 1781, the British were expelled by Spain and that country again assumed possession of Florida. In a very few years the inability which Spain has ever shown to properly govern her Colonial possessions was manifest. A war broke out between the Spaniards and the Seminole Indians of Florida and soon the whole State was in a condition of virtual anarchy. Emboldened by their successes in warfare, the Indians molested the frontier of Georgia. The Government of the United States then took an action which constituted a precedent for its action in invading Cuba in the late war with Spain. It despatched a military force into Florida under command of General Andrew Jackson. He virtually took possession of Florida and speedily restored order. His conduct excited much debate in Congress and in the Cabinet, a strong anti-expansion sentiment developing. The matter was finally settled by purchasing Florida from Spain for $5,000,000. This was done in 1819. Emigration poured into the territory from the States further north and soon the value of Florida as an acquisition to the country became evident and the anti-expansion sentiment died away. In 1845 Florida was admitted into the Union as a State. In 1861 it seceded with other Southern States and returned again to the Union in 1868.

It may be pertinent right here to say that when the United States buys or comes into possession of a tract of land it becomes the property of the country and is called a Territory, and under the Constitution it is so treated, without representation in Congress until such time as it is admitted into the Union and becomes one of the United States.

5

TEXAS.

This great Territory comprising 370,472 square miles originally belonged to Mexico. In 1820 Moses Austin, a native of Connecticut, obtained a grant of land and threw it open to settlement by people from the United States, mostly the Southern States. In a few years more than 20,000 had settled there and the strong Anglo-Saxon spirit of liberty began to rebel against the oppressive Mexican rule. In a few years this feeling burst into an open revolt. Texans met and declared their independence and formed a Republic and placed an army in the field under Gen. Sam. Houston. He met the Mexicans under Gen. Santa Anna at San Jacinto in 1836 and gained a complete victory, thus achieving the independence of Texas. Next year Texas applied for admission into the Union but no action was taken by Congress for several years. Meantime in the north a strong sentiment had developed against the institution of slavery. The subject was vigorously agitated in the pulpit, in literature and in public. The Southern people, perceiving the strength of the opposition to their favorite institution, determined in self defense to acquire more territory for the sake of the strength additional votes would give them, and so in 1844 the proposal to admit Texas came up in Congress in earnest.

No concealment of the underlying purpose was made by the Southern Congressmen who led the movement. A bitter struggle followed but the annexationists prevailed and in 1845 the "Lone Star State," as Texas had been called, was added to the Union. The South welcomed the new comer with great demonstrations, but the greetings of the North were not cordial, for in that section it was clearly understood that a great extension was given to slave territory.

NEW MEXICO AND ARIZONA.

The vast territory included in these two Territories was acquired mostly from Mexico in 1848 as one of the terms of the treaty of peace between the United States and that country made after the war of 1846-47. The war with Mexico was brought about by the refusal of the Mexican Government to concede the claims of Texas to land between the Rio Grande and the Nueces Rivers. The actual rights in the case were somewhat obscure, but war was eagerly undertaken by the Southern people, who believed that a further extension of slave territory would be the ultimate result. The North was less enthusiastic, for this reason, but sent a quota of troops into the field before whose valor, directed by commanding officers who later became prominent in the great war of the Rebellion, the Mexican armies were defeated. The United States paid Mexico $15,000,000 for the territory ceded under the treaty and in addition paid $3,500,000 in settlement of the claims of private individuals. The boundary line remained in dispute for five years more, until 1853, when James Gadsden negotiated a treaty with Mexico settling all questions. Under its terms the United States gained the Mesilla Valley, forming the southern part of what is now New Mexico and Arizona, and comprising 20,000,000 acres. The United States paid Mexico $10,000,000 for this land which was afterwards known as the Gadsden purchase and is so marked on the larger maps issued by the Interior Department at Washington. Including the territory acquired by the Mexican war, the State of Texas and that included in the Gadsden purchase, the whole area is sufficient to make one hundred and seventy States the size of Connecticut.

CALIFORNIA.

This great State was ceded to us by Mexico, being part of
that country before the war. In 1848 gold was discovered by
Capt. Sutter in a river near Sacramento. On examination gold
was found to occur in abundance. News of the wonderful
discovery drew an immense emigration into California from
all parts of the world, the majority of those traveling across
the plains by the way of the Isthmus of Panama being, of course,
from the United States. The people who poured into the golden
State lost no time in applying for admission into the Union.
In 1849, one year after Sutter's discovery, the State presented
itself at the door of Congress. In 1850 California was admitted.
The celerity of the operation was due to the fact the North
recognized, that California would offset to an extent the growth
of slave territory actually made by the admission of Texas and
threatened in Arizona and New Mexico, areas peculiarly adapted
by climate and other conditions to the institution of slavery.

Oregon, Washington and Idaho were part of what was called
the great Oregon country. They were acquired under an agreement with Great Britain in 1846. The United States claimed
the territory up to the parallel of 54° 49', but a compromise
was made and the 49th parallel accepted as the dividing line
between the United States and the British possessions. The
country north of the line is now known as British Columbia.

ALASKA.

Alaska, whose area is equal to about 120 States the size of
Connecticut, became the property of the United States in 1867
by purchase from Russia. The sum paid for it was $7,000,000.
The purchase, negotiated by Secretary of State Seward, was de-
nounced by many as an extravagant use of public funds because Alaska appeared to be practically worthless. The Gov-

ernment, however, unheeding the kind of criticism paid $200,000 in addition to the first price named to extinguish the rights of various commercial companies and thus acquired a clear title. It was soon found the supposed ice bound land was full of wealth in fisheries and lumber, the income from seal fisheries alone amounting in one year to $2,500,000. Alaska's wealth in gold was, however, not suspected until recent years and not demonstrated until the summer of 1896, when the now famous treasure ship arrived in San Francisco having on board over $600,000 in gold, the property of 50 prospectors who had washed it out of the bars of the creeks emptying into the Yukon river. Alaska, the "ice bound, inhospitable desert of the north," as it was designated in 1868, was a Mecca for the world for the next few months and thousands braved the dangers of Chilkoot pass to search for the yellow metal, and at this time it is estimated over 50,000 people are in that part of the Territory which two years ago was practically uninhabited.

GENERAL GRANT ON EXPANSION.

President Grant in his second inaugural address, March 4, 1873, thus expressed himself: "I do not share in the apprehension held by many as to the danger of governments becoming weakened and destroyed by reason of their extension of territory. Commerce, education and rapid transit of thought and matter by telegraph and steam have changed all this. Rather, I believe that our Great Maker is preparing the world, in his own good way to become one nation, speaking one language, and when armies and navies will no longer be required."

HAWAII, CUBA, PORTO RICO, AND THE PHILIPPINES.

These great and interesting acquisitions to our territory have not yet entered the blue field of our flag. To a great nation and to a humane people they will look for that protection which has been pledged to them; and if it is decided that these people shall live under our starry flag, no one can look back over its history and doubt the strength and breadth of its folds.

THE SOCIETY OF THE CINCINNATI.

This historic and patriotic order was named after the famous Roman Dictator and Patriot, Cincinnatus, and was founded in May, 1783, on the banks of the Hudson, by the American and French officers who had gathered there at the close of the Revolutionary war.

The resolution adopted at the forming of the society contained these words: "To perpetuate, therefore, as well the remembrance of this vast event as the mutual friendships which have been formed, of common danger, and, in many instances, cemented by the blood of the parties, the officers of the American Army do hereby, in the most solemn manner, associate, constitute and combine themselves into one society of friends to endure as long as they shall endure, or any of their eldest male posterity, and in failure thereof the collateral branches who may be judged worthy of becoming its supporters and defenders."

Owing to the great distances between the different States, and the fact that at that time the means of transportation were slow and uncertain, it was deemed best to form societies in each of the thirteen States. This was done. One was also organized in France under the patronage of Louis XVI.

The original members included the names of Washington, Greene, Hamilton, Lafayette, Rochambeau, and Paul Jones; in fact, all the historic military and naval characters of the Revolution. Among the honorary members elected for their own lives only were the names of many signers of the Declaration of Independence.

On the pages of the country's history appears no darker

spot than that placed there by the Congress of the United States
in its failure to give its soldiers the promised half pay for their
services, forcing them to leave their homes and emigrate to
the wild lands west of the Alleghenies, which were given to
them in lieu of money.   On this account several of the orders
in the different States went out of existence.

The patriotic societies of the country, the names of which
are given here, were all formed for the purpose of perpetuating
the memory of events and of the men who in military, naval
and civil positions of high trust and responsibility, "kept step
to the music of the Union."

The preservation of historical records and manuscripts and
the promoting of fraternal intercourse among their members are
the main inspirations of all of these patriotic societies:

Society of Colonial Wars.

Sons of the Revolution.

Society of the Sons of the American Revolution.

Military Order of the Loyal Legion of the United States.

Grand Army of the Republic.

Sons of Veterans U. S. A.

There are three great patriotic societies, organized by the
women of America, known as the Daughters of the Revolution,
Colonial Dames, and the Mayflower, that may outstrip all other
societies in the value and importance of their work.

DATES OF ADMISSION OF THE STATES.

Delaware, Dec. 7, 1787.
Pennsylvania, Dec. 12, 1787.
New Jersey, Dec. 18, 1787.
Georgia, Jan. 2, 1788.
Connecticut, Jan. 9. 1788.
Massachusetts, Feb. 6, 1788.
Maryland, April 28, 1788.
South Carolina, May 23. 1788.
New Hampshire, June 21, 1788.
Virginia, June 25, 1788.
New York, July 26, 1788.
North Carolina. Nov. 21. 1789.
Rhode Island. May 29. 1790.
Vermont. March 4. 1791.
Kentucky, June 1, 1792.
Tennessee, June 1. 1796.
Ohio, Feb. 19, 1803.
Louisiana, April 30, 1812.
Indiana, Dec. 11, 1816.
Mississippi, Dec. 10, 1817.
Illinois, Dec. 3, 1818.
Alabama. Dec. 14, 1819.
Maine. March 15, 1820.

Missouri, Aug. 10, 1821.
Arkansas, June 15, 1836.
Michigan, Jan. 26, 1837.
Florida, March 3. 1845.
Texas. Sept. 29, 1845.
Iowa, Dec. 28, 1846.
Wisconsin, May 29. 1848.
California. Sept. 9. 1850.
Minnesota, May 11, 1858.
Oregon, Feb. 14. 1859.
Kansas, Jan. 29. 1861.
West Virginia, June 19, 1863.
Nevada, Oct. 31. 1864.
Nebraska, March 1. 1867.
Colorado, Aug. 1, 1876.
North Dakota and
South Dakota, Nov. 2. 1889.
Montana, Nov. 8, 1889.
Washington. Nov. 11. 1889.
Idaho, July 3, 1890.
Wyoming. July 10, 1890.
Utah, 1894.

DATES OF ORGANIZATION.

Arizona, Feb. 24. 1863.
Alaska, July 27, 1868.
Indian Territory, June 30. 1834.

Oklahoma, April 22, 1889.
District of Columbia. March 3, 1791.
New Mexico, Sept. 9, 1850.

Commodore Perry carried our flag in 1854 into the harbors of Japan, and the first commercial treaty with that nation was made by and with the United States.

SAVE THE OLD FLAG HOUSE.
THE HOME OF BETSY ROSS.

The objects of the American Flag House and Betsy Ross Memorial Association are to purchase and preserve the historic building, situated at No. 239 Arch Street, Philadelphia, Pa., in which the first flag of the United States of America was made by Betsy Ross and subsequently adopted by Congress, June 14th, 1777, and to erect a national memorial in honor of this illustrious woman.

All loyal American hearts will welcome the glad tidings that active steps have been taken to purchase the birthplace of the Star Spangled Banner, and under the auspices of the American Flag House and Betsy Ross Memorial Association shall henceforth be preserved as a lasting tribute to those whose heroism resulted in establishing that freedom which a united people are to-day enjoying.

Appreciating the importance of preserving this relic of the Revolution, a number of patriotic gentlemen of this and other States have taken the matter in hand, thus making the movement national in its scope.

Numerous attempts have been made in the past to remove this historic building to other cities. The present plans provide that it shall remain in Philadelphia, where it rightfully belongs, there to be held in trust for the nation.

It has been left to the option of the American people whether the birthplace of their national emblem shall be permitted to pass into oblivion.

This landmark should be the mecca and shrine of the whole nation. It was associated with one of the most memorable incidents of our early history, and it is most fitting that it should be preserved for future generations.

Like "Independence Hall," wherein the Declaration of Independence was signed, and Faneuil Hall, the cradle of liberty, it speaks most eloquently of the men and women to whom we owe our freedom.

While we honor the heroes of the past, let us not forget to preserve the mementoes associated with them. Such relics increase in value as they are transmitted from one generation to another and form object lessons in history.

To follow our flag from its birth until to-day would be to write a history which stands absolutely alone, and from the day of its creation to the present time it has never trailed in the dust, being the only exception among the flags of the world. It is not that we have not been called upon to defend it and the underlying principles for which it stands, for to-day as we celebrate the anniversaries of victories on land and sea we cannot but recall, with mingled pride and pleasure, the achievements won under its glorious folds, and when our patriots, inspired by a Godlike devotion to flag and country, performed deeds of daring that mark their efforts as the most signal ever accomplished under any flag by any heroes of any nation.

With all these glorious deeds, and others that must necessarily follow, let us as a grateful, patriotic people see to it that the birthplace of our nation's flag be preserved as a holy shrine.

With the view of making the movement a popular one, arrangements have been made to have all Americans, of every shade of religious and political opinion, affiliate alike, and by their participation to become the preservers of the birthplace of the "Stars and Stripes."

On these broad principles souvenir certificates of membership in this Association will be issued at a nominal price, and the names of all subscribers placed on the roll of honor.

Any person desiring to see the Old Flag House saved and Betsy Ross honored may become a member of the "American Flag House and Betsy Ross Memorial Association" upon the payment of 10 cents, for which they will receive a beautiful certificate of membership, sixe 11x14, duly signed by the officers of the Association, and bearing the seal and certificate number. Upon these certificates in the centre is artistically portrayed the room in which Betsy Ross displayed the first Stars and Stripes to the committee appointed by Congress, consisting of General Washington, Robert Morris and Hon. George Ross. On the left is an exterior picture of the Old Flag House as it stands to-day, while on the right is the picture of the grave of Betsy Ross, at Mt. Moriah Cemetery.

These certificates will be mailed to any address upon the receipt of 10c.

NOTICE.

A large reproduction, in ten colors, size 22x28 inches, of the original painting, "Birth of Our Nation's Flag," by Charles H. Weisgerber, first exhibited at the World's Columbian Exposition, Chicago, 1893, will be presented as a souvenir to any person forming a club of thirty members, inclusive. These premium pictures will not be for sale, and when the objects of the Association are attained the plates will be destroyed; thus

they will become a valuable family heirloom. For upon them will be
engrossed the name of the individual forming the club, as follows:

"Presented to .... of ....
by the American Flag House and Betsy Ross Memorial Association, for
aiding in the preservation of the Birthplace of our Nation's Flag, and
for the erection of a National Memorial in Honor of Betsy Ross, and
stamped with the seal of the Association."

The picture referred to above is an exact representation of the room
in which the first American Flag was made by Betsy Ross, which was
subsequently adopted by Congress, June 14, 1777, and is the only endorsed portrait representation of Betsy Ross by her living descendants.

Address all communications to

JOHN QUINCY ADAMS, Secretary,
Old Flag House, 239 Arch Street, Philadelphia, Pa.